Easter
Coloring Book for Kids

Neil Masters

Copyright 2015

All Rights reserved. No part of this book may be reproduced or used in any way or formor by any means whether electronic or mechanical, this means that you cannot recordor photocopy any material ideas or tips that are provided in this book.

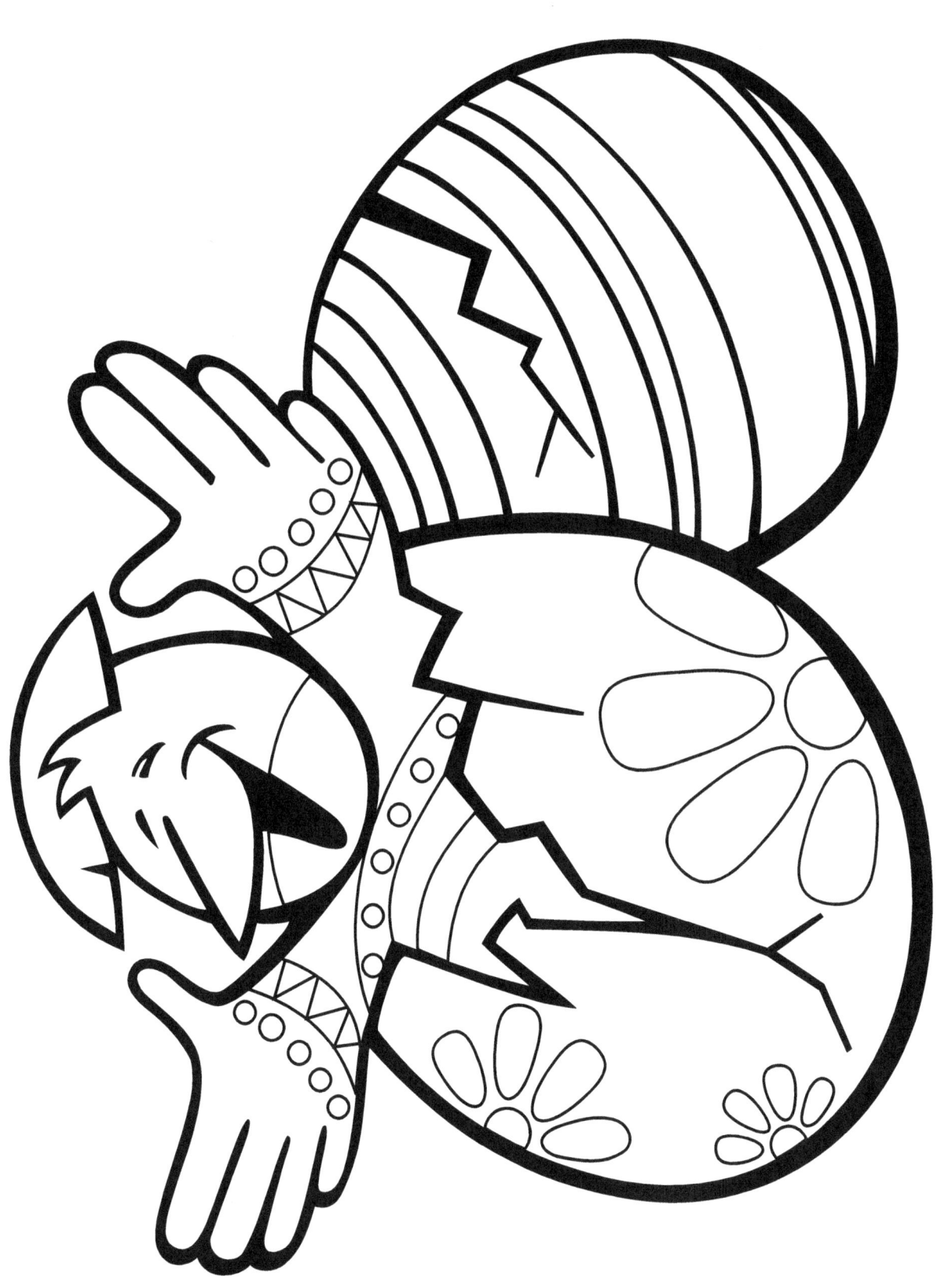

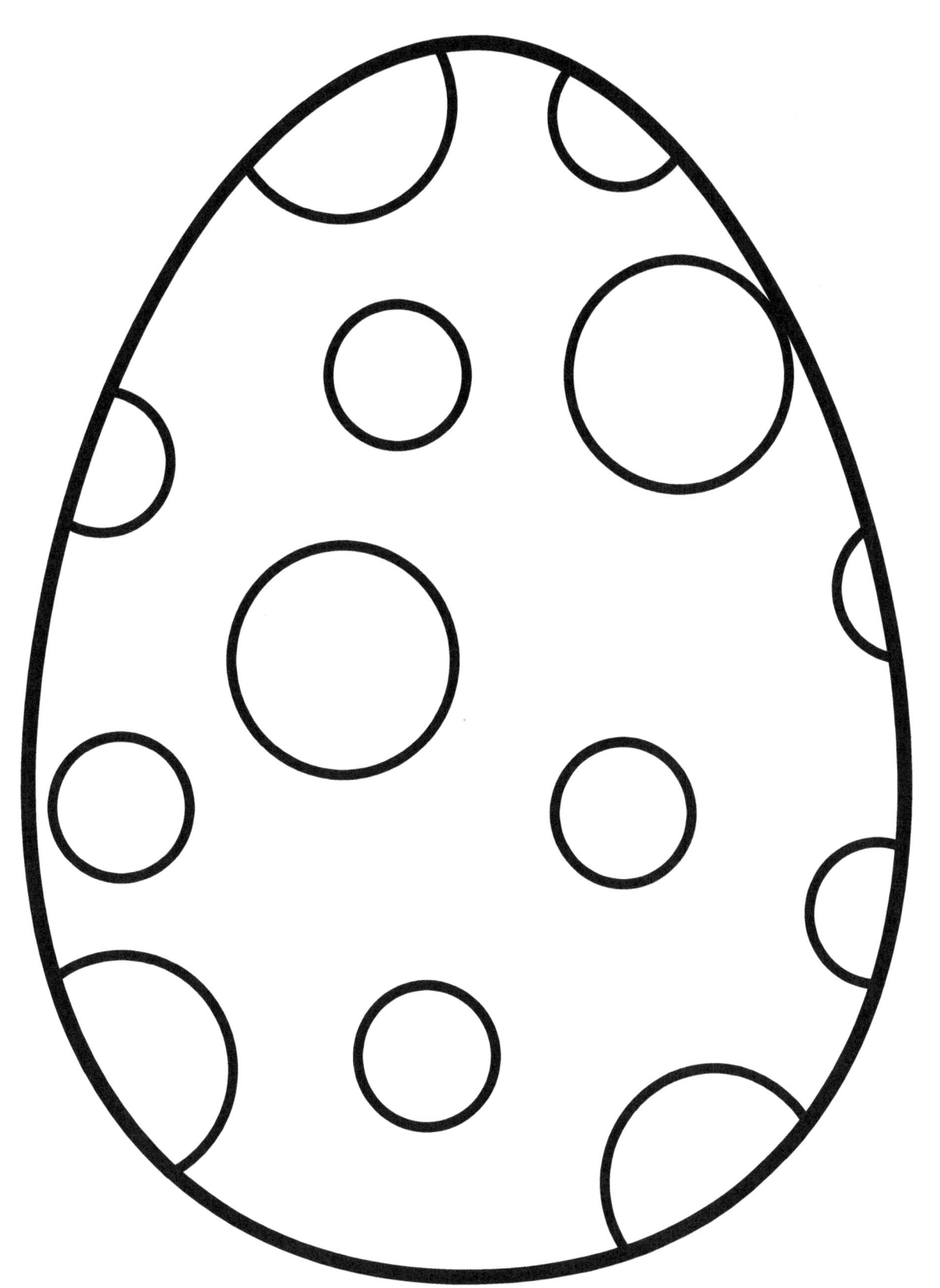

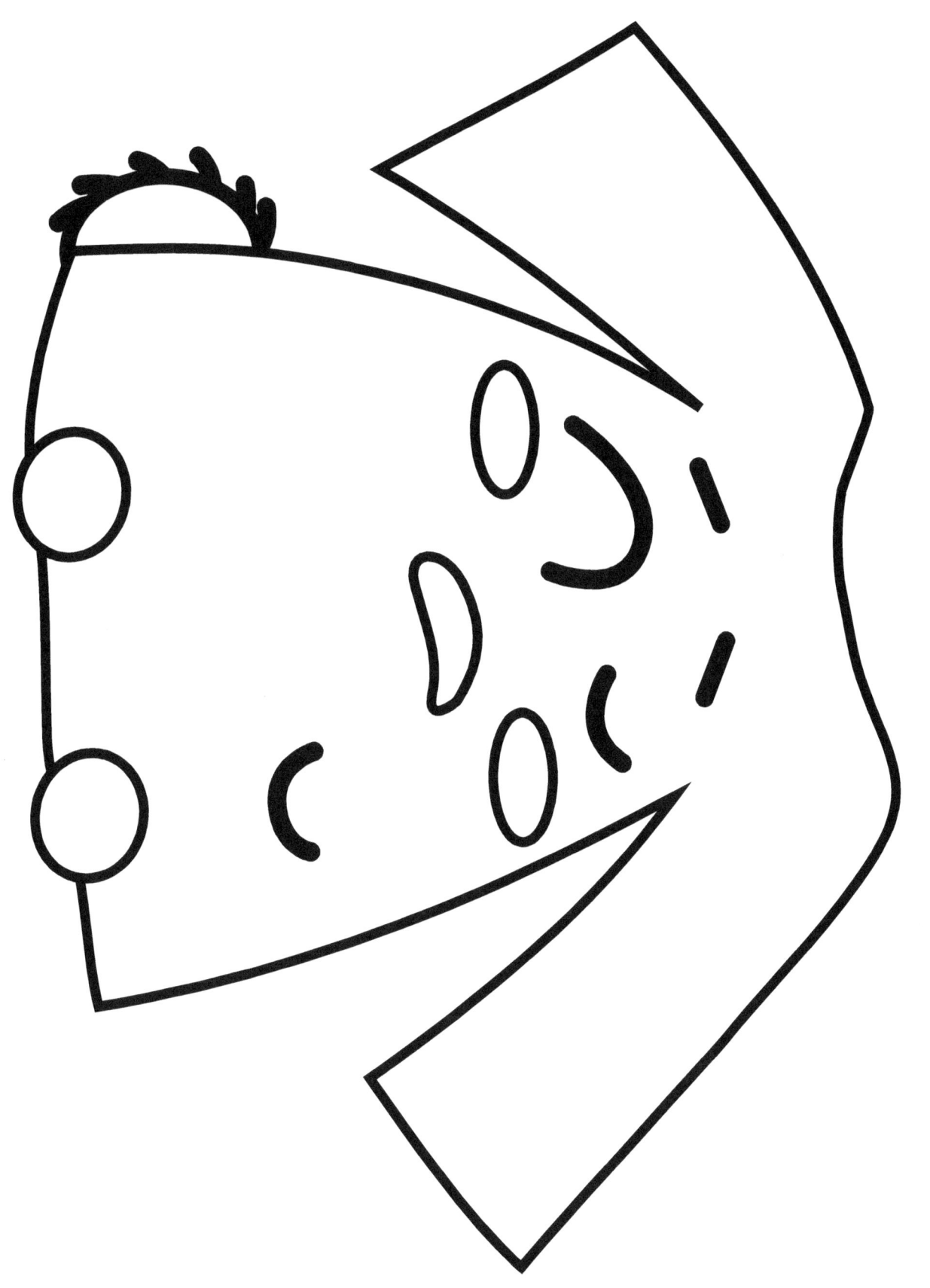

Happy Easter

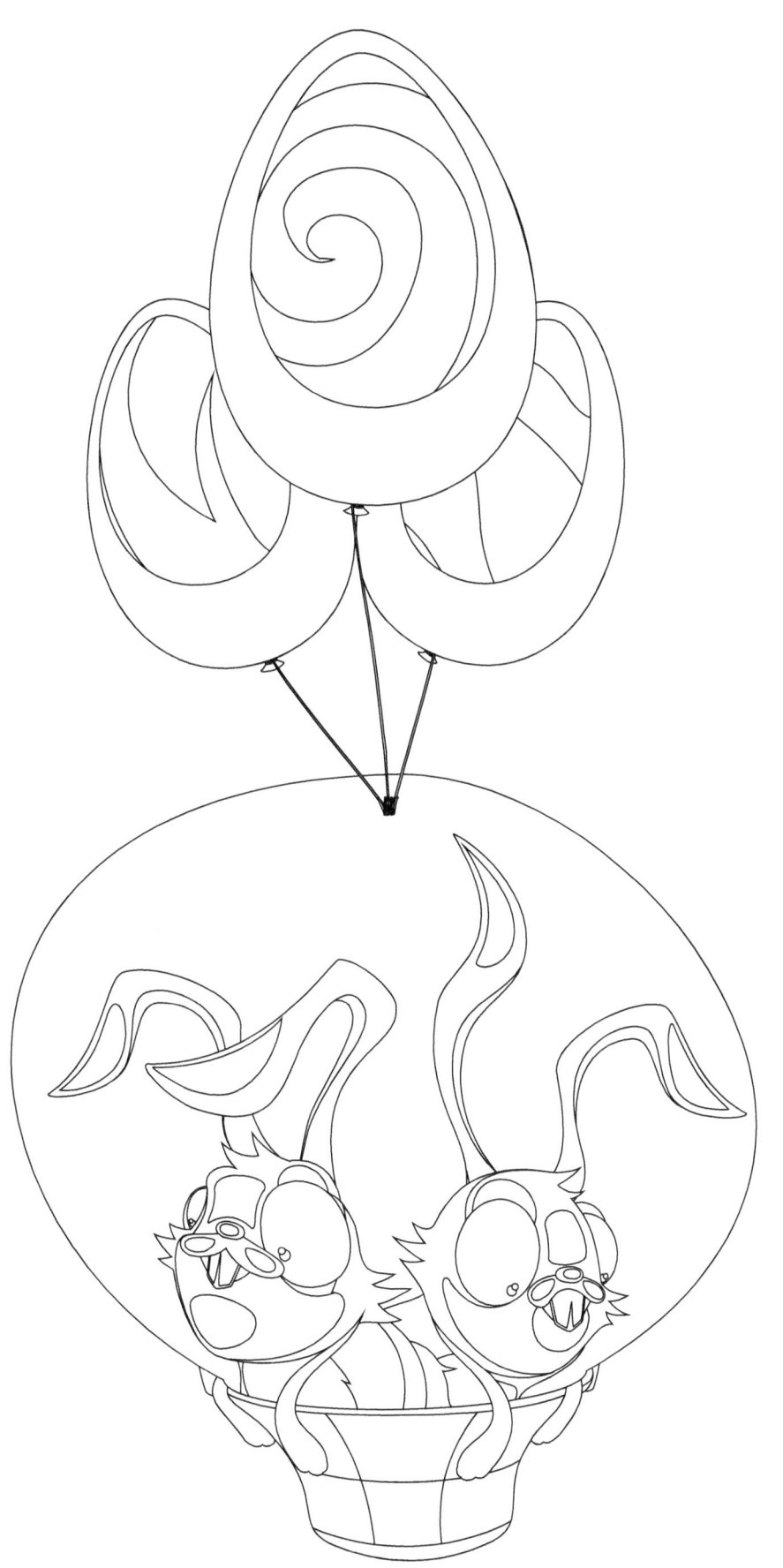

www.ingramcontent.com/pod-product-compliance
Lightning Source LLC
LaVergne TN
LVHW081543060526
838200LV00048B/2191